Dark Energy

D1253495

SPENCER CO. LIBRARY
168 TAYLORSVILLE RD.
TAYLORSVILLE, KY 40071

Also by Robert Morgan

POETRY

Zirconia Poems

Red Owl

Land Diving

Trunk & Thicket

Groundwork

Bronze Age

At the Edge of the Orchard Country

Sigodlin

Green River: New and Selected Poems

Wild Peavines

Topsoil Road

The Strange Attractor: New and Selected Poems

October Crossing

Terroir

FICTION

The Blue Valleys

The Mountains Won't Remember Us

The Hinterlands

The Truest Pleasure

Gap Creek

The Balm of Gilead Tree: New and Selected Stories

This Rock

Brave Enemies

The Road from Gap Creek

NONFICTION

Good Measure

Boone: A Biography

Lions of the West: Heroes and
    Villains of the Westward Expansion

Dark Energy

Robert Morgan

SPENCER CO. LIBRARY
168 TAYLORSVILLE RD.
TAYLORSVILLE, KY 40071

PENGUIN POETS

PENGUIN BOOKS   •

Published by the Penguin Group
Penguin Group (USA) LLC
375 Hudson Street
New York, New York 10014

USA | Canada | UK | Ireland | Australia | New Zealand | India | South Africa | China
penguin.com
A Penguin Random House Company

First published in Penguin Books 2015

Copyright © 2015 by Robert Morgan
Penguin supports copyright. Copyright fuels creativity, encourages diverse voices,
promotes free speech, and creates a vibrant culture. Thank you for buying an
authorized edition of this book and for complying with copyright laws by not
reproducing, scanning, or distributing any part of it in any form without permission.
You are supporting writers and allowing Penguin to continue to publish books for
every reader.

Page xi constitutes an extension of this copyright page.

LIBRARY OF CONGRESS CATALOGING-IN-PUBLICATION DATA
Morgan, Robert, 1944–
[Poems, Selections]
Dark energy / Robert Morgan.
pages ; cm.—(Penguin Poets)
I. Title.
PS3563.O87147A6 2015
811'.54—dc23
2015003965

Printed in the United States of America
10 9 8 7 6 5 4 3 2 1

Set in Fairfield Light   •   Designed by Ginger Legato

For my grandson Jamie

SPENCER CO. LIBRARY
168 TAYLORSVILLE RD.
TAYLORSVILLE, KY 40071

• CONTENTS

ONE

Big Talk   3

Big Bone Lick   4

Jaguar   5

Ancient Talk   6

Endowments   8

Canebrake   10

Carpet Tacking   11

Semper Fi   12

Flush   13

Log Tote   14

Teeth of Time   15

Abandoned   16

History   17

TWO

The Road to Arcadia   21

Going West   22

Even Me   23

High Horse   24

Heaven's Gate   25

Drag Harrow   26

Equinox   27

Escape Route   28

11/22/13   29

Cold Friday II   30

Fall   31

A Kind of Sacrament   32

THREE

Heartbreak and Flight   35

Cloud Farm   36

Clockwork   37

Chance   38

New Year   39

Be Drunk   40

Love Sleep   41

Doloroso   42

Left Behind   43

Aspen Song   44

Maple Gall   45

Living Tree   46

Valley Wind   47

Duty   48

Binary   49

Chinquapin Hill   50

Air Plant   51

Prodigy   52

Spit Bugs   53

Late Bloom   54

Ascent   55

Toothmarks   56

Locusts   57

Ancient Script   58

Morning Vision   59

FOUR

Noble Metals   63

Shelter   64

Periodic Table   65

Algae   66

Dark Matter   67

Parhelion   68

Rare   69

Substation   70

Milkomeda   71

Zircon   72

High-Tension Lines   73

Engine   74

Coriolis Effect   75

MRI   76

Widdershins   77

Neutrino   78

Dark Energy   79

Silence   80

• ACKNOWLEDGMENTS

I would like to thank the editors of the following journals for first publishing many of these poems: *Appalachian Heritage, Appalachian Journal, Asheville Poetry Review, The Atlantic, Badlands, Bat City Review, Congeries, Georgia Review, Hampden-Sydney Poetry Review, North Carolina Conversations, Now & Then, Southern Cultures, Southern Poetry Review, Southern Quarterly,* and *The Yale Review.*

"Ancient Talk" was first published as a broadside by the Thomas Wolfe Society.

"Living Tree" was published as a broadside by the North Carolina Writers Conference.

Special thanks to Cynthia Chase, Rebecca Godwin, Jesse Graves, William Harmon, Michael McFee, and Paul Slovak for their editorial wisdom.

Dark Energy

ONE

Big Talk

When mountains boomed and boomed again
returning echoes all along
the chain, the Indians said the peaks
were talking to each other in
the idiom that mountains use
across the mighty distances,
with giant syllables and rests.
White hunters feared it might be guns
or even cannon natives had
somehow acquired to warn them from
the better hunting grounds and streams,
the blasts as loud as thunder on
the clearest days and coldest nights.
Geologists would later hold
the groans and barks inside the ridge
were shelves of massive, restless rock
that slipped or dropped far down within
the mountain's guts, a fracture or
a crashing at some fault as part
of the tectonic conversation
among the continents as old
as planet earth or starry birth,
the gossip of creation's work.

Big Bone Lick

At Big Bone Lick the first explorers
found skeletons of elephants they said,
found ribs of woolly mammoths,
tusks of mastodons and ribs of sloths
that lurched across Kentucky once
near twenty feet from snout to tail.
They dug out teeth the size of bricks
and skulls of giant bison, beavers.
In salty mud licked bare by elk
and deer and buffalo and bears
for ten millennia, the bones
seemed wreckage from a mighty dream,
a graveyard from a golden age,
or killing ground of titans. Here
they saw the ruins of a world
survived by its diminutives,
where Eden once gave way and shrank
to just a regular promised land
to fit our deadly, human scale.

Jaguar

Where Lawson, Bartram, others wrote
they saw a "tiger" in the hills
and woods of Carolina I
assumed they meant a panther or
a bobcat, never guessed there were
American jaguars in these parts.
They named the Tyger River, built
a town called Tigerville. Turns out
they told the truth: the leopards they
recorded were inhabitants
and natives to these mountain heights,
had golden hair and spots and faces
like tigers of the Old World tales,
the metaphysical beast of Blake,
were strong enough to kill a horse
if other, smaller game was scarce.
It's something to consider, that
such speed and power and prowess once
patrolled these forests, mated, drank
from creeks and branches, screamed afar,
where fastest killer's now the car.

Ancient Talk

The story goes that Thomas Wolfe,
when touring the majestic West,
once stood before a great sequoia
for minutes that stretched to an hour,
as though communing with the soul
and roots and monolithic height
of the largest living thing on earth.
We know by then Wolfe had become
inspired by landscapes of the plains
and chains of higher mountains that
could dwarf his native Blue Ridge hills.
Colossus of a man himself,
he clearly felt a bond with peak
and pass and mighty glaciers,
with Rockies and the High Sierra,
with lofty meadow, alpine lake,
and timberline and grizzly bear.
He'd always been a listener
to what folks said or didn't say,
in Asheville, Harvard, New York too.
But now he was attentive to
the land, the forest, wind, and lore
of native history and craft,
the ancient talk of waterfall,
of aspen tree and mountain air.
He filled a notebook with his thoughts
and observations. Yet because
he was struck down so soon we don't

know what he learned from the sequoia.
Before that wisdom could be fixed
in words and narrative he had
been taken from our mortal sphere.
His gift to us, I think, is the
suggestion that we find our own
communion with the noble trees
and rocks and diamond peaks, and pause
to see and listen to the whisper
of our now fragile hemisphere.

Endowments

The families on the Oregon Trail
(as sun crashed down or wind slapped dust
in eyes and mouth and oxen strained
and hesitated hour by hour
along the rivers, over hills
and prairie grass, or lightning whipped
the air or hail flew level as
a volley of white musket balls,
and many burned with fever in
the wagon beds, some weakened by
starvation or bad meat, or cup
of poisoned water, and diseases passed
along the train, sometimes a raid
at dawn or bite of rattlesnake)
lost so many, so many died,
they quickly buried them in sod.
Atop the makeshift grave they stood
a wooden chair back like a sign.
The question later asked was why:
did chair back symbolize a bit
of culture in the endless wild,
a memory of the life back east?
Or was it more a sign of rest,
of dignity on alien land
after the horrendous journeying?
With rocks so few as well as trees
the chair back may have been the one
substantial thing they had to mark

the site and claim the soil above
the dear deceased, against the wolves
and time's predation, while they
must labor on, but leave behind
an artifact of comfort and
familiarity to keep
the vigil as a monument
on earth they'd never see again.

Canebrake

The fertile valley floors first seen
by Europeans flourished with
tall cane stalks twenty feet or more,
the home of panthers, rattlesnakes,
and calving bison cows and wolves.
The mighty grass would sway and rasp
and whisper far above the men
who ventured there in search of game.
A giant grove, a forest raised
so tall a human felt no more
than mouse or rabbit trapped within
the cage of stalks. But hunters found
a spark set to the cane would send
a whoosh of flame through canopy
in riot that would leave a ghost
of ashy curls across the acres,
and soon the brakes were just a scar
and then a memory, and then
not even that, as vanished as
the pigeon, panther, painted face.

Carpet Tacking

Back when whole communities gathered
to raise a barn, shuck corn, kill hogs,
shell peas, or spread manure on fields,
they sometimes would collect to tack
a neighbor's carpet down. The new
made rug was rolled up on the porch.
The front room must be emptied out
then swept and mopped and dried. And when
the mat and carpet were unscrolled
across the floor, each took a hammer,
a mouth of tacks called brads or sprigs,
and knelt along the edges of
the cloth to hold the fabric tight
and flat. They tapped a tiny nail
twice every inch to make the rug
lie straight and sure. The many hands
pinned down the fabric in an act
of social unity, the whole
community, and when the tacks
were firm they moved the chairs and table
back inside and ate the feast
prepared before. The room was bright
and fresh and newly soled and clean.
Laborare est orare
St. Benedict had said: "to work
is to pray." But these folks knew
a motto too, that when they worked as one
"to work is play" was also true.

Semper Fi

A hunter in the wilderness
accompanied by a faithful dog,
when struck by heart attack or stroke,
might lie for days in pain and fear.
The loyal dog stayed near and proved
a comfort to the fallen scout.
He licked the master's hand and lay
close by to keep the sufferer warm.
And when the hunter died the dog
kept vigil by the corpse for days
and warned away all predators,
and howled at stars and whined with grief.
Then as the body cooled and firmed
and ripened with decay the pet
remained on mournful guard. But as
the stage of putrefaction came
the final act of fealty was
to feast upon the dear cadaver
in last communion with the master.

Flush

A common sight in graveyards in
the countryside's the sunken grave.
Though times may vary in each case
the average age for graves to cave
is roughly half a century.
To compensate old folks would curve
the dirt in mounds above the site.
But after several years the box
below gives way and heavy earth
subsides, to settle, crush the whole
container of remains, the dust
of the beloved, as clay unites
with clay. And what is seen above
in turf's a new depression near
the stone, a pool of absence filled
by rain or snow or blowing leaves,
replacing loss of human earth,
until the spot is flush again
with hill and wind and planet's curve.

Log Tote

Crosscut saws and heavy axes
fought the trees along a boundary,
ate the hundred-year-old poplars,
tumbled twelve-foot-thick rock maples,
hollow sycamores like castles.
Once the trees were all reclining
and the sun reached forest litter,
drying moss and bleaching leaf rot,
it was time to stack and burn all
in a giant conflagration.
Logs that lived a half millennium
rolled to heaps and set ablazing
lit the firmament with roaring,
lifting higher than the trees had.
Round the fire the families frolicked,
roasted deer and passed the brandy.
Fiddle music sparked the dancing
near the fire big as a palace.
Young eyes met and romance started
in the heat from mighty timbers.
Songs were shouted at the night sky.
Those who stepped into the darkness
saw the fires on other mountains,
glow of dying forests' embers
reaching far into the future.

Teeth of Time

We know that candles weren't allowed
in medieval scriptoria—
all copying must be done by day,
by light available in cold
short winter shifts or summer's full.
The cause was not that candles might
drip sperm on vellum purity,
but fear of fire consuming both
the copied and the copy and
the whole library, borrowed, bought,
and made, illuminated texts
kept there for dusty centuries,
the manuscripts unique and true,
and guarded from mildew and grime
and minute worms called teeth of time.

Abandoned

Because the weeds rear up around
them, sheds abandoned seem to sink
into the very earth, the eaves
almost in contact with the brush
and thistledown of goldenrod
singed black by frost. The ridgepole droops
and shingles wear soft pads of moss.
The vegetation floods and swirls
around the leaning structure as
if eating wood, digesting logs,
absorbing frame and fabric in
the long assimilation of
all art into the hungry maw
of time, to be the compost we
can call collective memory.

History

Where cloudbursts tore a gash
in the shoulder of the ridge,
uprooting ferns and hedge,
a maple and an ash,
a honeysuckle vine
and wires of gold ground pine,
the slide exposed a vein
of mica, groundhog den,
a zone of luminous clay,
revealing rocks like teeth,
a seam of yellow earth,
and brought to light of noon,
after half a millennium,
there in the mud, a shining
coin of the Spanish king.

TWO

The Road to Arcadia

When I was stubborn at the age
of two or three, refusing to
lie down for nap or rest—my play
too colorful and various,
too dissonant and multiple
to turn away from, time too rich
with possibility to yield—
my mother knew just what to do.
She'd take a seat beside the fire
and pat her lap and start to sing.
It could be any song at all,
a hymn, or carol, Stephen Foster.
I can't explain the powerful pull,
the magnetism of her voice.
But dropping what I had I ran
to lay my cheek against her chest
and feel the notes through air and flesh,
the measure of the heart itself,
and drift away on melody
to my particular arcady.

Going West

When I was young I thought
if I could walk to the horizon,
go all the way, that I'd be free.
Beyond would be a different world
with different trees and different paths
and different animals and toys.
If I could only get away
and keep on walking I'd arrive
where everything was new, where sun
would plunge below to swim around
and reappear behind to soar
again, and rivers bubbled from
their seeds and rainbows could be touched
and followed to their treasure hoards.
All would be possible if I
just got beyond the garden fence,
beyond the hedge, beyond the river,
beyond the ridge, beyond my languor.

Even Me

When I was less than five years old
I sat beside a power line pole
that stood just at the edge of yard,
all black and scabbed and creosote tarred.
The shaft reached higher than the trees
and smelled of bitter chemistries.
And then I heard a choral hum,
a deeper bass than I had known.
With ear to wood I listened long;
the note went on and on and on.
Was music coming from the ground,
or from the pole so high in wind?
Or was the song from the big wires
that stretched like strings of a guitar
across the road and pasture hill?
There was no breeze that I could feel,
just tension in the wood and cable,
the guy wire pinned in nearby stubble.
The hymn went on, the voice of steel,
of sky and light and woods and field,
the voice of time from the beginning,
before a pulse or heart was beating,
the sound of space beyond the stars
and in between the atoms' spheres,
a voice of primal harmony,
still audible to even me.

High Horse

Where ice once pushed a black pine down,
or partly down, to lean askew
among the other pines along
the pasture edge, I liked to climb
upon the tilted trunk and ride
as if it were a rough bark steed.
With limbs for reins in hand I bounced
and made the tree sway up and down
as in a gentle canter. I'd
outrun the breeze and afternoon,
a jockey on a Thoroughbred,
a cowpoke on his quarter horse,
an Indian on a spotted pony.
I raced so far above the ground
it seemed I might take flight and rise
into the clouds and far above
the weather, whipping bark for speed,
more speed, as though on Pegasus
or chariot of Elijah heaven bound.
There seemed no end to galloping
and my exuberance until
I tired and chose to alter course,
and backed down off the too high horse
to set my feet on unmoved ground.

Heaven's Gate

In her nineties and afraid
of weather and of falling if
she wandered far outside her door,
my mother took to strolling in
the house. Around and round she'd go,
stalking into corners, backtrack,
then turn and speed down hallway, stop
almost at doorways, skirt a table,
march up to the kitchen sink and
wheel to left, then swing into
the bathroom, almost stumble on
a carpet there. She must have walked
a hundred miles or more among
her furniture and family pics,
mementos of her late husband.
Exercising heart and limb,
outwalking stroke, attack, she strode,
not restless like a lion in zoo,
but with a purpose and a gait,
and kept her eyes on heaven's gate.

Drag Harrow

A frame with teeth to comb the dirt
in spring, the harrow wears away
the clods and curries soil to look
as groomed and soft as corduroy.
And if you stand upon the bars
the spikes cut even deeper, rake
the lumps of sod. Around around
you go, avoiding apple trees,
the horse a little rusty from
his winter's rest. Worms glisten in
the furrows, birds swoop down to feast.
The field will shine with its new brushing,
the oaks electric gold with budding,
the sky above both cool and wide
as you glance up from clod to cloud.

Equinox

My great-great-grandpa thought the bull
was in the lower pasture but
he didn't know the fence was down.
He took a walk along the creek
to find a pocket of white clay.
He needed just a taste of that
to tone his system for the spring,
get rid of winter thickness, thin
his blood and limber up his joints.
It was an annual ritual.
It was the very afternoon
of equinox, frost gone from banks.
He felt the rush of sap in trees,
in roots of grass, in his own veins.
He couldn't hear the mutter of
the stream in flood, a robin's call,
or snort of his own Hereford
which ran behind with lowered head
and lifted him through air and light,
through blur of coming seasons to
the blinding center of the sun.

Escape Route

When Daddy drove his pickup truck
south from the hills, across the Piedmont,
to Greenville, South Carolina, he
took care to park on the north side
of town, the truck already aimed
toward home. And though he thrilled to crowds
and stores at first, to spectacle,
electric buses, higher buildings,
a hotdog at a diner, clothes
from finer haberdasheries,
he soon grew tired, within an hour,
or three, and was elated to
retrieve his truck still pointed at
the distant range, and freedom from
congested, smelly streets. Escape route
clear in mind, he raced along
the boulevard and shed the crush
of town, toward higher, cleaner air,
the intimate familiar.

11/22/13

Fifty years ago today
I sat in Joseph Flora's class
at Chapel Hill while he described
the First World War and Hemingway.
The clash of war and love was dire.
But we had leisure to discuss
the ravages in calm discourse.
The world had certainly improved
in half a century. And then
a student in the back who held
a tiny radio called out
"The president is shot." We sat
all stunned and scared and quiet till
Joe Flora said, "That goes to show
there's still much evil in the world."
And later as I walked across
the quad in balmy autumn light
I thought this was the end of our
good times, of something big. A way
of being confident had ended.
The air was punctured like a bubble
and there was no more oxygen.
The holiday parade was stopped
on Franklin Street, and youth was stopped.
The path ahead touched anger, fear,
through broken glass, hysteria.
Somehow the world had gotten bigger,
though life itself was smaller, meaner.

Cold Friday II

My grandpa never ceased to tell
the story of Cold Friday. He
would spit into the fireplace, reach
into his pocket for his knife
and start again the narrative
about the day the sun did not
appear. The chickens never left
the roost. It was so dark at noon
he had to work by lantern light.
The smoke from chimneys plunged to ground,
and cold contracted, drew away
the heat from fireplace, kitchen stove.
The lamps were lit at dinnertime
and cattle wouldn't leave their stalls.
Birds clung to limbs, refused to fly.
The mountains shrank beneath the clouds;
the mill wheel locked in fangs of ice.
Dogs hid themselves in cellar gloom.
Perhaps it was the end of time,
the Tribulation of the lost.
At least it seemed that time had stopped,
left human life in outer dark.
And then that night a high wind screamed
and morning sun found time redeemed.

Fall

The orchard my great-grandpa set
stretched up the pasture hill almost
to the golden grove of hickories.
There terraces were neat as stairs,
the trees in rows as though aligned
for roll call, mostly apples but
some pears and plums, and also cherries,
and many different strains, Ben Davis,
Delicious, Granny Smith, Winesap.
The colored fruit was bright and thick
as ornaments on Christmas trees.
The weeds on every tier were trimmed
and cushioned falling fruit. The fence
kept cattle out, protected quail
and other nesting birds. The gate
swung easy as a parlor door.
But after he was gone the trees
succumbed to weather one by one,
to time and blight and parasites.
The terraces decayed and blurred
in brush and hillside wash, the plot
returning to the looseness of
the wild, with briars and honeysuckle,
a garden of Edenic sprawl,
the hickories above still tall
as clouds, majestic in the fall.

A Kind of Sacrament

As a child I was intrigued
by swollen veins on the cow's udder.
It was a mystery how blood
could be transformed to milk. And yet
the rich and foaming drink was made,
so clearly was a product of
those warm and puffy passageways,
it seemed a miracle at hand
like water turned to wine. It was
a daily alchemy that made
of milk a kind of sacrament,
reversing the usual course
from mother's milk to sacrifice.

THREE

Heartbreak and Flight

A seed's a kind of Houdini
that, locked inside its jacket, all
contorted in a fetal knot,
is buried in obscurity.
Then moisture in the soil around
and sunlight on the ground above
stir something in the quickened heart
to make it split apart and thrust
a tentacle to push itself
heartbroken into April light,
and, shoving earth aside, it springs,
a phoenix form newborn and white,
to face the sun with spreading wings.

Cloud Farm

On this high slope in spring and fall
the wind's too vigorous for all
the usual crops like corn and beans,
the frost too late in May, the freeze
too early in September. Trees
get twisted, stunted by the smack
of the prevailing rhetoric,
though grass does pretty well and rocks
poke through the dirt like fossil stocks
of prehistoric orchard plots.
And weeds do business all around
the boulders, outcrops, scrubby growth.
But what thrives best on this high ground
is mist, the fogs that brood like ghosts
of ancient prophets on this height
so far above the fertile flats,
the vapors bright as angel wings
in fever dreams. Therefore this summit's
at best a farm for dreaming.

Clockwork

The sleet is fine as jewels in a watch
and clicks on leaves almost as regular
as ticks inside a fancy timepiece,
and snowflakes spin their interlocking gears.
Time's arrow seems to point into the clouds
and whitened ground appears to levitate.
The seconds count off yet another year
advancing toward infinity, which we
will never see but still can contemplate,
inside the clockwork of creation
in steady progress toward oblivion.

Chance

We feel the volt inside our veins,
inside the vines, inside the rain,
and through the capillaries of
a tree. We feel the pulse above
in storms, vibrato of thunder,
the whispering rhythms of a river,
magnetic currents in the earth,
the alternating flow of breath,
the push of tides, reversing air
from caves, dilating hum and dance
of bees, the chant of auctioneer.
All oscillate together, or
they seem to, in this play of chance,
beneath the stars' indifference.

New Year

The snowy field is pure and blank,
a page unwritten on, intact,
intimidating with its white
unblemished possibility,
and promise of the fresh, unknown.
All limbs are finned by mounting snow,
and snow's so deep the fence posts wear
tall dunce's caps, for storms this big
are just a kind of carnival,
flakes drifting like confetti, trees
pristine in costumes, and the snow
like makeup smoothing ditch and rut,
the clutter swept beneath, the mud
and trash all whitewashed over
and broken things immaculate
in bandages. All wait the grime,
the wound, the signature of time.

Be Drunk

The way a maple bleeds in spring
from cracks in shaggy bark you'd think
it was the never-healing wound
of Homer's poor Philoctetes.
Yet flies and moths and gnats go wild
to swill the suppurating wet
that looks like discharge from a toilet.
But touch the glistening seepage slick
as slime and taste the sugar from
the deepest roots, the sweetness just
a little bit fermented now
in hotter days, and see that what
you thought was just some horror of
decay is more a fountainhead
and flowing breast for orgy, yes,
a Dionysian feast and dance
to celebrate the day's abundance.

Love Sleep

Near dawn the katydids are quiet,
the rage and revel in the trees
along the ridge all done. All night
the rock and roll, the call for love,
the yearning blast and melody,
the torch song flowing on and on.
But now the woods are hushed with rapt
expectancy, the wait, the pause
of forest bowers exhausted by
a night of partying, a night
of romance in the leafy heights.
Now is the time for loving sleep,
and deeper dreams, of drifting on
through dark, before the rapture sun.

Doloroso

Why one rock in the path is damp
and other rocks around are dry
is something of a mystery,
like virgin statues that can cry
or saintly hands that bleed from scars.
Perhaps this kind of stone absorbs
and sweats the moisture of the air.
Or could the stone be deeper set
and keep the cool of undersoil,
the chill of earth, so long and well
that condensation gathers on
the face exposed to summer heat?
Therefore it is the depth and weight
that make this one stone weep, the size
that mocks the sadness of the wise.

Left Behind

When half the mighty willow fell,
broke off and crashed into the field,
it seemed ironic that it was
the living half the wind struck down.
The side left standing was all dead,
a skeleton of scaling bark
with pecker holes like marks of war.
You'd think the living half would be
the part most likely to survive.
The dead side might have crumbled long
ago. But living leaves resist
the wind and bear the brunt and lash
and tangle with the storm and take
the punishment to hold their foils
against an angry hurricane.
And now both sides are dead except
the longer dead still stands, goes on
for years perhaps, so lean, alone.

Aspen Song

The sound of water in the air
cools even summer sunlight,
as though the upland pasture
remembers oceans at this height
when even dirt and rocks were young
(warm-blooded life had just begun).
The breeze plays leaves in sweetest treble
and never tires of its long fable,
in counterpoint to human foible.

Maple Gall

What looks at first like rotten fruit,
hung round the maple's slender trunk,
we know's a tortured cluster of
malignancies where cells grow drunk
with larvae, mites or fungus, worms,
with virus or bacteria,
and multiply as tumors, bulge
of goiters, awful excess growths.
But when you look at all the gross
disfigurements at closer range
you see the beauty of distortion,
the sculpture of disease, the strange
and replicating work the tree
is not supposed to yield, a flowery
production so grotesque it seems
a kind of miracle in wood
that makes this sapling both unique
and memorable by virtue of
its suffering swollen sores and scars,
the warts that are its finest art.

Living Tree

It's said they planted trees by graves
to soak up spirits of the dead
through roots into the growing wood.
The favorite in the burial yards
I knew was common juniper.
One could do worse than pass into
such a species. I like to think
that when I'm gone the chemicals
and yes the spirit that was me
might be searched out by subtle roots
and raised with sap through capillaries
into an upright, fragrant trunk,
and aromatic twigs and bark,
through needles bright as hoarfrost to
the sunlight for a century
or more, in wood repelling rot
and standing tall with monuments
and statues there on the far hill,
erect as truth, a testimony,
in ground that's dignified by loss,
around a melancholy tree
that's pointing toward infinity.

Valley Wind

I reckon everybody knows
the pleasing breeze that tends to flow
up slopes on sunny summer days,
as air that's warmed by solar blaze
reflected lifts up valley sides
and stirs the leaves on towering heights,
a manic rise, a thrill of breath
to soothe the sweltering aftermath
of steady glare. Then as the sun
goes down the wind reverses run,
depresses slow then gathers speed
to sink from peak to valley bed,
the highs now balanced by the sloughs,
chill air from summit altitudes
and stratosphere pushed down
to cool the dew on bottom ground,
promoting sleep in house and den,
in burrow, nest at meadow's end,
the wind itself bipolar,
as many things we know are.

Duty

When turkeys peck in grass and weeds,
beaks hammering at soil as they
step left and right and back in some
elaborate dance, there's one among
the flock with head held high, as though
in vigil, on alert, while all
the others feast and forage toward
the unexamined ground. But wait,
the sentinel begins to peck
as well, except you notice now
another bird has raised its head
to scan the field for predators,
to listen maybe for a pack
of coyotes, duty passed
in some obscure rotation of
civilian trust, responsibility.

Binary

Two yellow butterflies go all
around above the weeds, across
the road, along the edge of trees.
They're up and down, beside, askew,
but always equidistant as
though tethered, in a fight or in
a dance. They ricochet and then
reciprocate; they fall and flit
aside, like twins or planets caught
in mutual fascination.
We know this is a ritual
of courtship, mating minuet,
these flowers that spin like particles
at love and matter's deepest core.

Chinquapin Hill

It was the chestnut blight that wiped
the chestnut's minor cousin out,
the sparkling chinquapin that once
spread over pasture lots, along
the edge of woods. The fruit
was small as berries, shone like gems
inside the spiky burs, each one
a morsel of wild taste, a pill
of concentrate nutrition. On
this high-above-the-river hill
the chinquapins grew near some graves,
of Cherokees the rumor was.
But now there's only this one bush,
a relic hidden in the brush,
but still producing every year
some drops of earlier terroir.

Air Plant

Like most great artists it must have
a patron, giant shoulders on which
to stand above the common clutter,
above the rotting mass and mud,
above the fray. And like a saint
or mystic thinker it can live
on air alone, on rain and sun
and understory shade, on wind
of total inspiration for
the nourishment of delicate
new colors, fresh exotic shapes
that mimic poisons, predators,
but draw the fertilizing bee.
Ascetic epicurean
on perch of elevated vision.

Prodigy

It is the strongest, tallest trees
that are most vulnerable to storms
and lightning's bite. The pine or oak,
the poplar goliath that soars
alone or far above the rest,
will catch the brunt of hurricane
or torch of electricity,
while lesser specimens in groves
protect each other mutually
achieving near immunity
as lofty loners far above
are taken down with awful crash
or blown to splinters by a flash
that leaves unharmed conformity
above the fallen prodigy.

Spit Bugs

The gobs on weeds at first appear
like tufts of wool or rabbit fur.
But closer up you see the drops
of foam, the liquid bubble wrap
the nymphs are insulated by,
like bits of froth flung from the sky.
The weeds would seem to be in bloom,
or else a field of ripe cotton.
But if you wait a few days' time,
a thousand wings will lift from slime.

Late Bloom

What seems the last purple aster
of the season's hiding in a ditch.
Protected there from frost it leans
head down, its loaded brush of color
still luminous below the freeze-
burned stalks. The one survivor shows
advantage of a low profile.
The humble near-the-ground position
among the refuse, dust, debris,
enables the longevity,
allows late-blooming splendor when
the higher, bigger kin have gone,
the lowest brighter now, alone.

Ascent

An eagle or a hawk that floats
so high above a mountain slope
can see the mice and shrews and moles
and other rodents far below
scurrying beneath the packed snow.
The raptor spies quick shadow
beads that dart and pause and follow
subnivian tunnels that burrow
deep under drifts and hollow
layers between ice that show
up as if lit by skylights. Mice go
about their business to and fro,
gathering seeds and buds and willow
roots until a shade blots out the glow
and claws tear through with mighty blow
to lift warm fur from frozen meadow
into the blazing wind's hello.

Toothmarks

Just looking at the scratches on
this rock, all cut the same direction,
you'd never guess the little scores
were tracks of mighty glaciers.
What seems the grooves of rake or comb
are traces of a crushing dome
that passed this way first going south
and then with thaw retreating north,
the work of far millennium
writ small as epitaph for tomb.

Locusts

What a surprise it is to hear
that locusts come the thirteenth year
and not the seventeenth as told
for ages and enshrined in old
folklore and rhymes and family lies.
The species similar otherwise:
cicadas books call periodic,
found here in our southern district.
They grow from eggs pressed into twigs.
The nymphs that hatch then start to dig
at least ten inches into soil,
and live by sucking juicy oil
from roots and stems, sweet sap
that nourishes through the giant nap,
and then the lucky thirteenth year
they grow a polished armor
and crawl into the summer air
and, louder than a Mahler choir,
fill meadow, hedge, and orchard grove
with necessary calls for love,
then leave their eggs to fortune's whim
with Philip Glass–like requiem.

Ancient Script

The crows in fields of snowy drifts
resemble black cuneiform,
perhaps a poem from the time
of Sumer or Akkad, a song
of winter's promised passing,
or some forgotten writ of law,
though all I hear is caw on caw,
and then the silence answering.

Morning Vision

The cobweb on the lawn is white
with dew at dawn, a handkerchief
dropped there in some forgotten game,
a sign, a souvenir of one
who passed here in the night the way
a queen might drop a scarf to be
retrieved by a favorite courtier.
The fabric is immaculate
until the sun cuts through the trees
and makes the cloth a page of light
as many colored as the sheet
of an illuminated text,
a hovering just above the grass,
as though a dove sent from the sun.
But later when you search the ground
just wisps and filaments are found,
and nothing of the morning vision,
though grass itself is tender green.

FOUR

Noble Metals

The metals we call noble won't
combine with other elements,
don't interact with water, air.
Of course that means they don't corrode
or fade or rust, need little work
of polishing. So gold and some
alloys and also platinum,
like minerals of Elysium,
remain aloof and scintillant,
keep their immunity to change
while ordinary iron will burn
in time, get eaten by the air
like living things that die and rot
and mingle with the fecund mold.
But platinum, its alloys, gold,
and all their noble kin, will hold
their purity like some ideal
of beauty, bright and sterile,
like everything immortal.

Shelter

The hammering on the barn next door
goes on and on hour after hour,
day after day. The knocks at first
like cracks and smacks become more blunt
and resonant as work proceeds
and blows made higher in the air
with walls to amplify the strokes
reach farther out across the field
between that place and here. The bangs
create accompaniment, a bass
of background drumming for our day,
not regular as pulse or heart,
but syncopated, fast at times
then slower and relaxed, a beat
that's tied to pace of effort as
the structure grows with every lick
and nail and shining piece of pine
to make a house for horses, hay,
as music makes a home in time,
each step of our long labor to
construct the fabric of a day.

Periodic Table

Is this the calendar of all
creation where each square within
the grid displays another stage
of rise or growth of matter out
of chaos, out of light, the bang,
as though the net of lines and signs,
in this reticulation, could
haul in the catch of time itself,
as if the specimens of mass
were blocks with labels printed on
to stack up neatly as the world
or chessboard of the elements,
the universe complete from birth
to scattered cinders at the end
beyond the death of energy,
in this one table of the whole,
or our conjecture of the all?

Algae

The stuff in ditches early spring
could be a luminous refuse,
the lumps and clots, the dumplings green
and golden, just the muck of life
in hairy chunks of phosphorescence.
It multiplies as mulch around
the roots of cattails, ferns, and reeds,
and thickens to a luscious paste
of photosynthetic essence
of tiny vegetables at base
of a gigantic food chain maze.
And floating free in slimy whirls
it shoulders up the living world.

Dark Matter

That what we know is just
a fraction of what is
is nothing new. The sense
of giant looming presence
beyond the human ken
is old as human thought
and human fear and love
and human celebration.
That what we touch and hear
and see is just the tip
of unseen realms and laws
may be the start of our
intelligence, may be
the launch of honest awe
and curiosity,
and lesson of humility.

Parhelion

Look up into the winter sky,
the air all clear to grape-black space,
except the ether is on fire
with needle ice and glitter rays.
And not a single sun you see,
but blinding, reigning trinity,
like three gold apples hung above
a pawnshop door, and making three
a sign of earth's depository
where something left can be redeemed.
They blaze until you look aside,
and then there's only one next time.

Rare

You must have seen the highest shelves
get little dust, though lower down
at each successive stage the soot
will thicken, catch like tawny frost
and build a loose velour on wood,
on books, on glass of paperweight.
And at the floor the drift is deep
as ancient tomb or desert ditch.
The dust is light as lint or ash
of time and mist of gnats and smoke,
a snow from Brownian turbulence.
But higher up the air is warm
and mostly free except for fumes
above the swirling particles
that swim in entropy's fine rain.

Substation

Is this a kind of church, out here
beyond the suburbs and beyond
the condominiums, but near
the shopping malls and trailer parks,
the lit-up towers and cables arcs
as steep as flying buttresses,
where giant messages come in
from over the horizon on
steel couriers shouldering mighty volts
to be translated here for use
in homes by ordinary folks,
transmitting and interpreting
the power for city's multitudes?
On lonely roads, in autumn rain,
transformers hum Gregorian.

Milkomeda

Predictions are that far away,
in years to come, our galaxy,
our shining Milky Way, will touch
and crash into Andromeda,
just several billion years from now.
When mighty wheels of stars collide,
they circle, hold each other in
a kind of dance, churn dust and gas,
and finally merge in one ellipse
of blazing light. The starburst whirl,
the turbulence of light and dark,
will be the nursery of the new
and growing planet systems far
into the future, spinning worlds,
enhancing possibilities for life
and extra-heavy elements,
restructuring the zodiacs
from marriage of giant snowflakes.

Zircon

When my great-uncles dug for zircons on
the mountainside and on the pasture hill
a hundred years ago they'd no idea
the little crystal bit they sought would be
a token from the planet's fiery birth.
For zircons are almost as old as earth's
creation in the conflagration from
debris that formed the galaxies of suns.
This tiny stone found in the family dirt's
a kind of clock they say, a register
of time from the beginning since it traps
uranium and other elements
decaying at a steady measured rate.
The zircon lasts when mother rocks around
have crumbled, worn away to sand. It keeps
the fingerprints of isotopes from clouds
of the original primordial dust,
right here where spiders hide in rotting duff.

High-Tension Lines

Like staves of music they are flung
from pole to pole outstretched across
the valley, up a hill, and swung
along the ridge. They shine with gloss
as bright as cobwebs in the sun
and seem as delicate as floss.
They reach the clearing near at hand
from source of generation,
through town and county, public land,
from distant power creation,
and sing the thrill of transmission.

Engine

A motor is a kind of god
with blood of grease and oil upon
its altar. We worship it with hands
and wrench, with sacrifice of sweat
and patience, many hours, and pour
libations and anointing drops.
And when we turn the switch and press
an otherworldly spirit sings
from deep inside the covenant
of steel, the ark of immanence,
with transcendental eloquence.

Coriolis Effect

Because the earth is made to spin
and tilted on its axis, none
can fall or travel in a line.
For everything that moves is swept
aside a little by the force
of planetary rotation.
We try to move directly toward
our object but find deviation.
There is no straight and narrow way,
just swerving routes, and twisting paths.
The place you aim for will be gone
before you reach there, for the world
we know, the only world we know,
is warped and sprung and devious
and turns its face away and throws
us off the chosen course and off
the goal, into the arc of gravity.

MRI

In this white crypt beneath a tower,
occult, immaculate, a drum
begins to send a warning from
the deep recesses of the walls.
And somewhere else a dove will call
across the mist. A morris dance
is under way. The pings and chants
of crickets, katydids, cicadas,
as summer reaches its hiatus.
The beat is now reflected in
the bone, the nerve, the flesh, the brain,
the bang of creation, doom,
the pulse of the original womb.
There is a drip, a tock, a groan,
and then a hammer on and on.

This is the rhythm avant-garde.
There is a ringing in the pipes
somewhere, a knock on wood, a tap
and flutter of percussion, zap,
and then machine gun fire on top
of shrieks, exotic birds that keep
the air alive as biddies peep
and sonar, in a trough as deep
as ocean cave, as rivers sweep
away detritus, shadows creep,
probes inner landscapes for a map,
the ghost of mind a snowy alp.

Widdershins

To go against the clock is sinister,
to turn always to left and left again
in circles toward the center just behind you.
They say that those bewitched go widdershins
as though the spell drew them away that would
walk straight ahead and sure. When trying to
go forward they will swerve and veer, are pulled
by unseen force away from purpose, away
into the shadow side as if to find
the other hand, the back, dark energy.
While thistle seeds fly off on broomsticks, milk
turns sour and won't make butter, won't come sweet,
the victim steps aside from the lean path
and walks astray, stride twisted by the haunt,
as if to find what can't be known or said
beyond the edge of what is seen or heard.

Neutrino

We are compelled to find
the smallest bit of matter,
creation's building speck,
and look into the vast
remoteness of the tiny,
beyond the cell, beyond
the molecule and gene,
beyond the atom with
its nucleus and rings,
electron moons, beyond
the particles, the quarks
with many flavors, to
the one elusive, last
and ultimate suspicion
of substance, so minute
it passes through the earth
untouched, unrecognized,
except it leaves a blink
of sparkle in the dark
of stillest water tank
in cave or mine, too faint
and quick to monitor
but for the instant glints
it strikes, creation's tracks
that flick and disappear.
We never actually see one,
just winks where it has gone.

Dark Energy

It's odd to think that empty space
between the stars and galaxies
produces a repulsive force,
that emptiness will push away
all matter it encounters with
some kind of antigravity.
For nature is supposed to hate
a vacuum and rush to fill
all space unoccupied and bare.
But in the greater distances
between the worlds it would appear
the opposite is true. For there
a different kind of nature seems
to fear the close attraction of
the heavenly bodies, repel
both neighbor and chance traveler,
expanding to infinity
the bits of dust and light we know,
in a disintegrating zero
drawn toward the outer silence.

Silence

The dialect of perfect calm.
The air is clean, immaculate,
and nothing moves but time itself,
a cool delicious element.
It is the stillness at the heart
of matter, eye of hurricane.
It is the pitch of poise, of stone
and total immobility.
It is the voice of thought alone,
the sound of wisdom's ponder weight.
It is the carol of immanence,
both pregnancy and aftermath.
It is the thrill of the neutrino,
the hush of the electrical
and anthem of deep space. It is
the idiom of promised rest.

PHOTO BY RANDI ANGLIN

Robert Morgan is the author of fourteen books of poetry, most recently *Terroir*, 2011. He has also published nine volumes of fiction, including *Gap Creek*, a *New York Times* bestseller. A sequel to *Gap Creek*, *The Road from Gap Creek*, was published in 2013. In addition he is the author of three nonfiction books, *Good Measure: Essays, Interviews, and Notes on Poetry*; *Boone: A Biography*; and *Lions of the West: Heroes and Villains of the Westward Expansion*. He has been awarded the James G. Hanes Poetry Prize by the Fellowship of Southern Writers, and the Academy Award in Literature by the American Academy of Arts and Letters. In 2013 he received the History Award Medal from the DAR. His play *Homemade Yankees* was awarded the East Tennessee Civil War Alliance John Cullum Drama Prize. Recipient of fellowships from the Guggenheim and Rockefeller foundations, the National Endowment for the Arts, and the New York State Arts Council, he has served as visiting writer at Davidson College and at Furman, Duke, Appalachian State, and East Carolina universities. A member of the Fellowship of Southern Writers, he was inducted into the North Carolina Literary Hall of Fame in 2010. Born in Hendersonville, North Carolina, he has taught since 1971 at Cornell University, where he is Kappa Alpha Professor of English.

JOHN ASHBERY
Selected Poems
Self-Portrait in a Convex Mirror

TED BERRIGAN
The Sonnets

LAUREN BERRY
The Lifting Dress

JOE BONOMO
Installations

PHILIP BOOTH
Lifelines: Selected Poems,
1950–1999
Selves

JULIANNE BUCHSBAUM
The Apothecary's Heir

JIM CARROLL
Fear of Dreaming:
The Selected Poems
Living at the Movies
Void of Course

ALISON HAWTHORNE DEMING
Genius Loci
Rope

CARL DENNIS
Another Reason
Callings
New and Selected Poems
1974–2004
Practical Gods
Ranking the Wishes
Unknown Friends

DIANE DI PRIMA
Loba

STUART DISCHELL
Backwards Days
Dig Safe

STEPHEN DOBYNS
Velocities: New and Selected
Poems, 1966–1992

EDWARD DORN
Way More West: New and
Selected Poems

ROGER FANNING
The Middle Ages

ADAM FOULDS
The Broken Word

CARRIE FOUNTAIN
Burn Lake
Instant Winner

AMY GERSTLER
Crown of Weeds: Poems
Dearest Creature
Ghost Girl
Medicine
Nerve Storm
Scattered at Sea

EUGENE GLORIA
Drivers at the Short-Time Motel
Hoodlum Birds
My Favorite Warlord

DEBORA GREGER
By Herself
Desert Fathers, Uranium
Daughters
God
Men, Women, and Ghosts
Western Art

TERRANCE HAYES
Hip Logic
How to be Drawn
Lighthead
Wind in a Box

NATHAN HOKS
The Narrow Circle

ROBERT HUNTER
Sentinel and Other Poems

MARY KARR
Viper Rum

WILLIAM KECKLER
Sanskrit of the Body

JACK KEROUAC
Book of Sketches
Book of Blues
Book of Haikus

JOANNA KLINK
Circadian
Excerpts from a Secret
Prophecy
Raptus

JOANNE KYGER
As Ever:
Selected Poems

ANN LAUTERBACH
Hum
If in Time: Selected Poems,
1975–2000
On a Stair
Or to Begin Again
Under the Sign

CORINNE LEE
PYX

PHILLIS LEVIN
May Day
Mercury

PATRICIA LOCKWOOD
Motherland Fatherland
Homelandsexuals

WILLIAM LOGAN
Macbeth in Venice
Madame X
Strange Flesh
The Whispering Gallery

ADRIAN MATEJKA
The Big Smoke
Mixology

MICHAEL MCCLURE
Huge Dreams: San Francisco
and Beat Poems

ROSE MCLARNEY
Its Day Being Gone

DAVID MELTZER
David's Copy: The Selected
Poems of David Meltzer

ROBERT MORGAN
Dark Energy
Terroir

CAROL MUSKE-DUKES
An Octave Above Thunder
Red Trousseau
Twin Cities

ALICE NOTLEY
Culture of One
The Descent of Alette
Disobedience
In the Pines
Mysteries of Small Houses

WILLIE PERDOMO
The Essential Hits of
Shorty Bon Bon

LAWRENCE RAAB
The History of Forgetting
Visible Signs: New and Selected
Poems

BARBARA RAS
The Last Skin
One Hidden Stuff

MICHAEL ROBBINS
Alien vs. Predator
The Second Sex

PATTIANN ROGERS
Generations
Holy Heathen Rhapsody
Wayfare

WILLIAM STOBB
Absentia
Nervous Systems

TRYFON TOLIDES
An Almost Pure Empty Walking

ANNE WALDMAN
Gossamurmur
Kill or Cure
Manatee/Humanity
Structure of the World
Compared to a Bubble

JAMES WELCH
Riding the Earthboy 40

PHILIP WHALEN
Overtime: Selected Poems

ROBERT WRIGLEY
Anatomy of Melancholy and
Other Poems
Beautiful Country
Earthly Meditations: New and
Selected Poems
Lives of the Animals
Reign of Snakes

MARK YAKICH
The Importance of Peeling
Potatoes in Ukraine
Unrelated Individuals Forming
a Group Waiting to Cross